£1-

THE TWELVE DAYS OF CHRISTMAS COOKBOOK

The Twelve Days of Christmas Cookbook

Ruth Moorman & Lalla Williams

QUAIL RIDGE PRESS

Lovingly dedicated to
Ney, John, Ney, Jr., Wickliffe,
Dudley, Randall, Harris

Other books by
Ruth Moorman and Lalla Williams:

The Seven Chocolate Sins
A Salad A Day

PREFACE

N addition to its being a great religious festival, Christmas in Christian countries has always been a time of festivity. Christmas Day and the eleven days following are traditionally party days, and it is the intent of this book to suggest ways in which those days may be celebrated.

As the title of the book suggests, the parties, more particularly the party menus, are based on the suggestions—some obvious, some, we admit, a little strained—contained in the familiar song:

> On the first day of Christmas. my true love gave to me,
> A partridge in a pear tree. . .

Thus, among a variety of suitable substitutions, "geese a-laying" is magically transformed into pâté and "five golden rings" into molded orange cream!

But the real usefulness of the book lies not in its party suggestions alone, but in its accumulation of recipes appropriate to the holiday season. They come from a variety of sources—family hand-me-downs, out-of-print cookbooks, reconstructed restaurant secrets, any number of people and places. But all have been tampered and tinkered with, tried again and again, and finally tasted and approved. The reader is encouraged to try her/his own embellishments.

The menus, like the recipes, can be freely altered. It would be sacrilege, of course, to move the three French hens to the fourth day, but one is not bound to serve calas and café au lait on the third day.

So, dear reader, Merry Christmas I through XII!

On the First Day of Christmas,

my true love gave to me, a partridge in a pear tree.

In addition to the traditional Christmas dinner menu, we offer one featuring quail—called partridge in some sections of the South. Happy is the cook who tries the sweet potato recipe; foresighted the one who makes the plum pudding!

CHRISTMAS DINNER

Turkey with Cornbread Dressing
Holiday Sweet Potatoes
Green Beans and Celery
Cranberry-Pear Salad
Golden Rolls
Pumpkin Pie
Plum Pudding with Hard Sauce

- or -

Quail
Dirty Rice
Broccoli Casserole
Parsleyed Carrots
Molded Cranberry Salad
Mayonnaise for Sure
Quick Yeast Rolls
Mincemeat Pie
Pears Joyeuses

ROAST TURKEY

Allow ¾ to 1 pound per serving. Clean thoroughly, rub with butter, season with salt and pepper and pack stuffing loosely. Place in a roasting pan with a small amount of water. Cover and bake at 350 degrees, allowing 20–25 minutes per pound. Uncover and bake at 500 degrees 15 minutes or until brown.

CORNBREAD DRESSING

1 (10-inch) skillet of cornbread
made day before from de-
sired recipe
4 slices stale white bread (French
bread is good)
1 stick butter
3 eggs

1 cup onion, finely chopped
1 cup celery, finely chopped
4 tablespoons parsley, minced
½ teaspoon sage (optional)
4 cups chicken broth
Salt and pepper

Crumble breads and mix together. In a heavy skillet, saute' onion and celery in butter until clear. Add chicken broth and simmer 5 minutes. Add parsley and pour mixture over bread. Mix well. Lightly mix in eggs. Season. The mixture should be soft, neither soupy nor dry. Add more broth if necessary. This may be baked in a casserole or muffin tins instead of in the turkey. If baked separately, bake at 400 degrees 45 minutes for the casserole, 20 minutes for muffins. Serves 6–8.

EASY CORNBREAD

¾ cup self-rising flour
¾ cup self-rising cornmeal
½ teaspoon baking powder
½ teaspoon sugar

¾ cup milk
1 egg, slightly beaten
2 tablespoons butter

Mix dry ingredients together. Stir milk into egg and blend into dry mixture. Melt butter in baking pan or skillet and pour into batter. Stir and pour into same pan and bake at 425 degrees 20 minutes. Serves 6–8.

First Day of Christmas

HOLIDAY SWEET POTATOES

A word about sweet potatoes. They are different sizes and so one needs to adjust the liquid measurements. They seem to absorb huge amounts of flavoring, so one must taste throughout the preparation.

6 large sweet potatoes, baked,
   peeled and mashed
3 eggs
1 cup milk
½ cup bourbon
1½ cups sugar

½ teaspoon salt
½ teaspoon cinnamon
1 teaspoon allspice
2 teaspoons vanilla
Marshmallows or grated orange
   rind

Mix all ingredients well, beating until light and fluffy. If there is need for more liquid, increase the bourbon as well as the milk. Bake in greased casserole at 350 degrees until set. Garnish with finely grated orange rind or cover with marshmallows and bake until marshmallows melt and begin to turn color. Serves 8—10.

GREEN BEANS AND CELERY

2 (16-ounce) cans or 2 packages
   frozen French-style green
   beans
¼ cup butter

1 stalk celery, cut diagonally
¼ cup celery leaves, chopped
1 (5-ounce) can water chestnuts
Salt and pepper

Cook beans according to directions (canned beans should be drained and cooked in fresh water). Drain. Melt butter in a large skillet and saute' the celery until clear. Add water chestnuts and leaves and cook until leaves are wilted. Stir in green beans. Season. Serves 8.

First Day of Christmas

CRANBERRY-PEAR SALAD

2 cups cranberries
½ cup water
1 cup sugar
1 teaspoon cornstarch

1 (8-ounce) package cream cheese
¼ cup milk
¾ cup chopped pecans
1 dozen pear halves

Cook cranberries in water and sugar until soft. Mash the berries and add the cornstarch dissolved in 2 tablespoons water. Stir until the syrup thickens and is transparent. Soften the cream cheese with milk and add the chopped pecans. Drain the pear halves and fill the centers with the cheese mixture. Spoon the cranberries over the pears, cheese side up, and chill. Serve on bed of lettuce. Serves 6.

GOLDEN ROLLS

½ cup sugar
¼ cup shortening
¼ cup soft butter
1 teaspoon salt
2 eggs, beaten
1 cup warm water

1 package yeast dissolved in
    3 tablespoons warm water
4 cups flour (2 unbleached,
    2 plain)
Melted butter

Blend sugar, shortening, salt, and eggs. Add 1 cup warm water. Stir in yeast mixture. Add flour and beat thoroughly. This dough can be refrigerated for several days or used the same day. If it is to be used the same day, let it sit at room temperature for 2 hours. About 2 hours before baking, roll out the dough on a floured board to ¼-inch thickness. Cut out with biscuit cutter. Brush with melted butter and fold over half the circle. Let rise for 2 hours. Bake at 425 degrees for about 8 minutes. Makes about 4 dozen.

PUMPKIN PIE

2 eggs
1 (16-ounce) can of pumpkin
¾ cup sugar
1½ teaspoons cinnamon
1 teaspoon allspice

½ teaspoon ginger
¼ teaspoon cloves
½ teaspoon salt
1 (13-ounce) can evaporated milk
1 (10-inch) unbaked pie shell

Beat the eggs slightly, stirring in pumpkin and adding sugar until blended. Add spices. Blend in milk. Pour into an unbaked pie shell. Bake 15 minutes at 425 degrees, then reduce oven to 350 degrees and bake for 45 minutes or until a knife blade inserted in center comes out clean.

PIE CRUST

¼ cup ice water
2 cups flour

1 teaspoon salt
¾ cup shortening

Put ice cubes in a glass of water. Add salt to the flour and cut in the shortening with a pastry blender. Add ¼ cup of ice water and stir with a fork until the dough forms a ball. Roll out. For a baked pie shell, prick the bottom of the crust several times with the tines of a fork. Flute the edge by pressing the index finger of one hand between the index and third fingers of the other. Bake at 425 degrees for about 15 minutes or until it begins to color. Recipe makes a double pie crust or 2 pie shells.

PLUM PUDDING

3 cups fruit (raisins, currants,
  citron, peel, figs)
¾ cup soft bread crumbs
½ cup flour
½ cup sugar
1 teaspoon mixed spices
  (pumpkin pie spice)

½ teaspoon nutmeg
¼ teaspoon cinnamon
¼ teaspoon salt
¾ cup butter, cut into small
  pieces
2 eggs, beaten
4 tablespoons brandy

Mix together dry ingredients. Stir in the remaining ingredients and mix thoroughly. Put into a greased earthenware bowl, cover, and steam 4 hours. Cool. Cover top with a piece of freezer paper, waxed side out, and then cover with a cloth. Store in a cool, dry place. Steam 2 hours before serving with Hard Sauce. Serves 8.

HARD SAUCE

1 stick butter
1½ cups powdered sugar

2 tablespoons brandy, bourbon,
  or rum

Cream butter and sugar. Add liquor.

ROAST QUAIL

6 birds
Lemon juice
Salt and pepper

1 stick butter, melted
¾ cup olive oil
1 cup dry red wine

Rub birds with lemon juice, salt and pepper. Coat with butter and oil. Place in roasting pan with small amount of water and the wine. Bake covered at 325 degrees for an hour, or until tender. Remove cover and baste thoroughly, then return to oven without the cover until brown. Serves 6.

DIRTY RICE

2 cups rice
2 small onions, chopped
4 green onion tops, chopped
1 tablespoon parsley, minced

2 chicken livers and gizzards,
  chopped
2 tablespoons butter
Salt and pepper

Cook rice in 4 cups lightly salted water. Sauté remaining ingredients in butter until done. Stir in rice. Season. Serves 6–8.

BROCCOLI CASSEROLE

3 packages frozen, chopped
  broccoli
1 stick butter
½ bunch green onions, chopped
  (tops, too)

½ cup celery, finely chopped
3 tablespoons flour
1 roll garlic cheese, cut up
1 can cream of mushroom soup
1 (4-ounce) can mushroom pieces

Cook broccoli according to directions. Drain. Melt butter. Sauté onions and celery until tender. Add flour and cook, stirring, for 2 minutes. Add cheese and stir until melted. Blend in soup. Add broccoli and mushrooms. Bake in greased casserole, covered, at 350 degrees for about 30 minutes, or freeze and bake at 375 degrees for about an hour. Serves 8–10. This can also be used as a dip.

PARSLEYED CARROTS

10 carrots, sliced
¼ cup butter
2 tablespoons lemon juice

1 tablespoon parsley, minced
½ teaspoon salt

Cook carrots until barely tender in a small amount of lightly salted water. Drain and add the other ingredients. Serve immediately. Serves 6–8.

MOLDED CRANBERRY SALAD

1 package lemon or orange
  gelatin
1½ cups cranberries, washed
1 orange, seeded and cut up

1 cup sugar
½ cup celery, finely chopped
½ cup pecans, chopped

Dissolve gelatin in ½ cup boiling water. Blend in a blender cranberries, orange, and sugar, and add to gelatin. Stir in celery and pecans. Chill until firm. Garnish with mayonnaise. Serves 8.

MAYONNAISE FOR SURE

2 egg yolks
2 cups oil
½ teaspoon prepared mustard

Juice of half a lemon or
  2 tablespoons vinegar
1 teaspoon salt

Mix mustard into egg yolks with a fork. Add oil a few drops at a time and beat with hand beater or mixer on slowest speed. As it blends, the oil can be added faster. When rather stiff, add the salt and liquid. Continue beating in the remaining oil. Makes one pint.

QUICK YEAST ROLLS

2¾ cups flour
1 teaspoon baking powder
1 teaspoon salt
1 cup buttermilk, lukewarm
1 package yeast

2 tablespoons sugar
¼ teaspoon baking soda
1 egg, beaten
3 tablespoons shortening, melted
  and cooled

Sift together flour, baking powder and salt. Dissolve yeast in warm buttermilk. Add sugar, baking soda, egg, and melted shortening. Mix well and add to dry ingredients, blending thoroughly. Shape into rolls and allow to rise 1 hour. Bake at 425 degrees for 15 minutes. Makes about 3 dozen rolls.

First Day of Christmas

MINCEMEAT PIE

Make double crust. Fill with prepared mincemeat. If dry mincemeat package is used, follow directions substituting 1 tablespoon brandy for 1 tablespoon liquid. Dot with butter and cover, fluting edges to seal and using a fork to pierce holes about 6 times. Bake at 450 degrees for 10 minutes and then at 350 degrees for 45 minutes or until done.

PEARS JOYEUSES

1 (29-ounce) can of pear halves   *Whipping cream*
2 tablespoons Cointreau

Remove pears from can. Cook syrup until thickened, then add Cointreau. Pour over pears and chill thoroughly. Serve with cream. Serves 6.

On the Second Day of Christmas,

my true love gave to me, two turtledoves.

The party appropriately is for two. Instead of turtle doves, the menus have turtle soup and doves or mock turtle soup and tournedos (close enough if one mumbles?). We suggest that you add sherry to canned turtle soup and garnish with slices of hard-cooked egg and lemon. Since the mock turtle soup takes a bit of doing and makes more than two servings, it should be made ahead and frozen with two servings in a separate container. The chocolate pie freezes well, and the apple will, too!

DINNER INTIME

Turtle Soup
Parsley Buttered Tournedos
Onions and Peas
Baked Potatoes
Green Salad
Hot Rolls
Chocolate Dream Pie

- or -

Mock Turtle Soup
Doves with Bacon
Cheese Grits
Green Beans Almondine
Avocado and Grapefruit Salad
Hot Rolls
Apple Pie 'a la Mode

TOURNEDOS

Tournedos is the upper tail of tenderloin. Broil as you do any steak. Garnish with a pat of parsley butter.

PARSLEY BUTTER

1 tablespoon butter
1 tablespoon parsley, minced

Few drops of lemon juice
Salt and pepper

Mix ingredients thoroughly and chill.

ONIONS AND PEAS

2 onions
2 teaspoons Worcestershire sauce
4 teaspoons butter
Salt and pepper

1 tablespoon butter
1 tablespoon flour
½ cup milk
1 (8-ounce) can small English peas

Peel and cut onions in half. Place, cut edge up, in a lightly greased casserole. Top each half with ½ teaspoon Worcestershire sauce and 1 teaspoon butter. Season. Cover and bake at 400 degrees for about 45 minutes or until done. (The time of baking will depend upon the size of the onions.) Make cream sauce with butter, flour and milk. Add drained peas and heat. Ladle over onion halves. Serves 2.

SALAD DRESSING FOR MIXED SALAD GREENS

¾ cup oil
2 tablespoons white vinegar (or
1 tablespoon white vinegar

and 1 tablespoon lemon juice)
Salt and pepper

Combine the ingredients in a jar and shake well. Store in refrigerator.

CHOCOLATE DREAM PIE

1 (9-inch) graham cracker crust
   (recipe follows)
4 ounces German sweet chocolate
2 tablespoons water
3 eggs, separated

Few grains salt
1 teaspoon vanilla
1 teaspoon rum flavoring
½ pint whipping cream, whipped
   and sweetened

Melt chocolate in water. Beat yolks until light, then beat in melted chocolate. Add salt to egg whites and beat until stiff. Fold into chocolate. Add flavorings. Pour into pie shell. Chill overnight or freeze. Serve with sweetened whipped cream.

GRAHAM CRACKER CRUST

9 graham crackers
2 tablespoons butter

2 tablespoons sugar
¼ cup pecans, chopped

Roll out crackers and mix in sugar, butter and pecans. Press into pie pan and bake at 400 degrees for about 5 minutes.

MOCK TURTLE SOUP

2 cups cooked chicken
4 tablespoons shortening
4 tablespoons flour
1 large onion, chopped
1 bell pepper, chopped
2 stalks of celery, chopped
1 clove garlic, minced
2 hard-cooked eggs
1 tablespoon oil
½ teaspoon ground cloves

½ teaspoon cinnamon
½ teaspoon nutmeg
1 (8-ounce) can tomato sauce
Broth chicken has been
   cooked in
1 bay leaf
1 sprig thyme
Salt and pepper
½ cup sherry
1 lemon

Cut chicken into small pieces. Brown flour in shortening. Add onion, bell pepper, celery and garlic. Cook, stirring, until vegetables begin to soften. Mash the yolks with the cloves, cinnamon, nutmeg, and oil. Blend in the tomato sauce, 1½ quarts liquid (broth plus hot water), bay leaf, thyme, egg yolk mixture, salt and pepper. Bring to a boil and then simmer for about an hour. Before serving add sherry and garnish each bowl with a slice of lemon and chopped egg white. Serves 8.

Second Day of Christmas

DOVES WITH BACON

Season doves with salt and pepper. Place a piece of bacon over the breast and broil.

CHEESE GRITS

1 cup grits
1 stick butter
1½ cups sharp Cheddar cheese, grated

3 eggs, beaten
¾ cup milk
½ teaspoon Worcestershire sauce
Dash of garlic salt

Cook grits according to directions. Stir in butter and cheese until melted. Add milk to eggs and stir well into grits. Add seasoning. Bake in greased casserole at 325 degrees for 1 hour or until set. This dish can be frozen before baked, so we suggest that you place enough for 2 servings in a small casserole and freeze the rest. The small casserole will cook in about 30 minutes. This recipe serves 6.

GREEN BEANS ALMONDINE

1 package frozen French-style green beans
1 tablespoon onion, minced
1 tablespoon butter
1 tablespoon flour
½ cup light cream

¼ cup Swiss or Cheddar cheese, grated
Tabasco
Salt and pepper
¼ cup almonds, slivered

Cook green beans according to directions. Drain. Saute' onion in butter until tender. Add flour and cook, stirring, 2 minutes. Add cream and cheese and stir until cheese melts and sauce is smooth. Add a few drops of Tabasco, salt and pepper. Stir in cooked beans. Pour into greased casserole, sprinkle almonds on top, and bake at 375 degrees for about 20 minutes. Serves 4.

AVOCADO AND GRAPEFRUIT SALAD

Avocados, peeled and sliced
Grapefruit sections (fresh)
Lettuce
¾ cup olive oil
Juice of 3 lemons
1 teaspoon salt

1 teaspoon dry mustard
1 teaspoon cracked pepper
1 garlic clove, crushed
1 teaspoon parsley flakes
¼ teaspoon paprika

Arrange avocado slices and grapefruit sections on a bed of lettuce on individual salad plates. Blend the rest of the ingredients to make the dressing. Pour the dressing over the salad.

APPLE PIE A LA MODE

1 (9-inch) single unbaked pie
    crust
6 cups sliced apples
½ cup brown sugar, firmly packed
¼ teaspoon cinnamon
1 teaspoon vanilla

¾ cup sugar
¾ cup flour
¼ teaspoon salt
2 tablespoons butter
Vanilla ice cream

Mix brown sugar, ¼ teaspoon cinnamon, and vanilla with apples. Put mixture into crust. Mix sugar, flour, other ¼ teaspoon cinnamon, and salt. With pastry blender or fork, blend in butter to make topping. Sprinkle topping over apples. Bake at 425 degrees for 15 minutes. Reduce heat to 350 degrees and bake for 25 minutes, or until topping is golden brown. Serve topped with ice cream.

On the Third Day of Christmas,

my true love gave to me, three French hens.

What about a "hen party"? Morning coffee for the "girls" is our suggestion. Everything except the doughnuts and calas can be made ahead. The calas must be begun the night before. Choose one or several of the goodies for your party.

MORNING COFFEE

Café au Lait
Calas
French Market Doughnuts
Cranberry Loaf or Muffins
Kentucky Bourbon Balls
Coffee Cheese Cake
Lemon Pound Cake
Chocolate Pound Cake
Cinnamon Coffee Cake
Danish

CAFE AU LAIT

Bring equal parts of coffee and milk to boiling point. Pour together into cup.

CALAS

3 cups water
½ cup rice
½ teaspoon sugar
½ tablespoon yeast
½ cup warm water
1 egg, well beaten

6 tablespoons plus ½ teaspoon
  sugar
¾ cup flour
½ teaspoon nutmeg
Shortening
Powdered sugar

Boil rice until very soft. Drain and cool. Mash well and blend in ½ teaspoon sugar plus yeast dissolved in warm water. Let rise overnight. Beat egg into rice. Add sugar and flour and beat thoroughly. Let rise 15 minutes. Add nutmeg. Drop by tablespoons in deep fat until golden brown. Drain and sprinkle with powdered sugar. Serve warm with Café Au Lait. Makes about 2 dozen.

FRENCH MARKET DOUGHNUTS

2 tablespoons shortening
¼ cup sugar
½ teaspoon salt
½ cup boiling water
½ cup light cream

1 package yeast
¼ cup warm water
1 egg, beaten
3½–4 cups flour

Add boiling water to shortening, sugar, and salt. Add cream and cool. Dissolve yeast in warm water and add to shortening mixture. Stir in egg. Beat in 2½ cups flour. Add flour to make soft dough. Place in greased bowl. Cover and chill. When ready to use, roll out to ¼-inch thickness. Cut into squares and fry in deep fat. Drain on paper towels and dust with powdered sugar. Makes about 3 dozen.

CRANBERRY LOAF

2 cups flour
½ teaspoon baking powder
1 teaspoon salt
½ teaspoon soda
1¼ cups sugar
1 orange, grated rind and juice

2 tablespoons shortening, melted
Boiling water
1 egg, lightly beaten
¾ cups fresh cranberries, chopped
½ cup nuts, chopped

Mix the dry ingredients, and add the grated rind of the orange. Squeeze the orange juice into a measuring cup. Add the melted shortening and then add enough boiling water to make ¾ cup liquid. Mix thoroughly with the dry ingredients. Blend in egg, cranberries, and nuts. Bake in a greased loaf pan at 350 degrees for 50—60 minutes. Do not overcook. The batter can also be baked in greased muffin tins at 425 degrees for about 20 minutes.

KENTUCKY BOURBON BALLS

2½ cups vanilla wafers, crushed
1 cup powdered sugar
1 cup pecans, finely chopped
2 tablespoons cocoa

3 tablespoons corn syrup
3 ounces bourbon (2 jiggers)
Powdered sugar

Combine first four ingredients. Dissolve syrup in bourbon and add to dry mixture. Form into balls, and roll them in powdered sugar. Store in tin for several days before serving. Makes about 3 dozen.

Third Day of Christmas

COFFEE CHEESE CAKE

1½ cups graham cracker crumbs
2 tablespoons butter
2 tablespoons sugar
½ cup plus 2 tablespoons sugar
2 tablespoons flour
½ teaspoon salt
2 (8-ounce) packages cream
   cheese

4 eggs, separated
1 teaspoon vanilla
2 teaspoons instant coffee dissolved in 1 teaspoon hot
   water
½ pint whipping cream
½ pint sour cream

Blend crumbs, butter and 2 tablespoons sugar, and press into bottom of 9-inch spring-form pan. Mix sugar, flour, and salt, and blend into cream cheese softened with 2 tablespoons of the whipping cream. Beat in egg yolks one at a time. Add vanilla, coffee, and remainder of whipping cream, and blend thoroughly. Beat egg whites until stiff and fold into cheese mixture. Pour into spring-form pan and bake at 325 degrees for an hour or until done. Cool before removing rim. Spread sour cream on top. Chill thoroughly before serving. Serves 12.

LEMON POUND CAKE

1 cup shortening
1¾ cups sugar
6 eggs
2 cups flour
½ teaspoon salt

1 teaspoon vanilla
2 teaspoons lemon flavoring
Juice of 1 lemon
2 tablespoons powdered sugar

Cream shortening and sugar. Beat in eggs one at a time. Add salt to flour and beat into mixture. Add flavoring. Bake in greased, floured, tube pan at 325 degrees for 1 hour and 15 minutes, or until done. Pour mixture of lemon juice and powdered sugar over cake as soon as it comes from oven.

CHOCOLATE POUND CAKE

1½ cups shortening (1 cup butter
   or margarine)
3 cups sugar
5 eggs
3 cups flour
½ teaspoon salt

½ teaspoon baking powder
½ teaspoon cinnamon
½ cup cocoa
1 cup milk
2 teaspoons vanilla

Cream shortening and sugar. Beat in eggs one at a time. Sift dry ingredients together. Beat in alternately with milk and vanilla. Bake in greased, floured, tube pan at 300 degrees for 1½ hours, or until done. Frost while cake is hot.

FROSTING

2 tablespoons cocoa
2 tablespoons butter
1½ cups powdered sugar

1 tablespoon milk
1 teaspoon vanilla
Few grains of salt

Melt butter. Blend in cocoa. Beat in sugar, milk, vanilla and salt.

CINNAMON COFFEE CAKE

½ pint sour cream
½ teaspoon baking soda
2 eggs, beaten
1½ cups flour

1 cup sugar
2 teaspoons baking powder
½ teaspoon salt
4 tablespoons butter, melted

Blend sour cream, baking soda and eggs. Sift together flour, sugar, baking powder and salt. Beat into egg mixture. Blend in melted butter and pour into greased 9-inch square pan. Sprinkle with topping. Bake at 425 degrees about 25 minutes or until done. Immediately drizzle glaze over cake.

TOPPING

Mix together:
2 tablespoons brown sugar
2 tablespoons butter
2 tablespoons flour
1 teaspoon cinnamon
¼ cup pecans, chopped

GLAZE

½ cup powdered sugar
1 tablespoon milk
¼ teaspoon vanilla

Dissolve sugar in milk and vanilla.

Third Day of Christmas

DANISH

2 cups flour
2 sticks butter
1 cup plus 2 tablespoons water
3 eggs

2 teaspoons almond flavoring
¼ cup sugar
Powdered sugar
Slivered almonds

Cut 1 stick butter into 1 cup flour. Add 2 tablespoons water and mix well. A few extra drops of water may be needed to blend the ingredients well. Divide the pastry in half. Pat each half into a portion approximately 12 inches long on a greased baking sheet. Heat 1 stick butter and 1 cup water to boiling. Add almond flavoring and ¼ cup sugar. Pour into a crockery bowl and add 1 cup flour. Blend well. Add the eggs one at a time, mixing well. Spread over the two halves of pastry. Bake at 350 degrees for 50—60 minutes, or until golden. Dust with powdered sugar and sprinkle with toasted, slivered almonds. Serves 8—10.

Third Day of Christmas

On the Fourth Day of Christmas,

my true love gave to me, four mockingbirds.

Isn't it a crime to kill one? We decided to concentrate on the first syllable in planning a dinner party; thus the birds are "mock" rather than "mocking."

DINNER

Veal Birds
Asparagus Loaf
Green Salad
Hot Rolls
Charlie's Chocolate Mousse
- or -

Blind Finches
Buttered Noodles
Creole Cucumbers
Mock Chicken Salad
Hot Rolls
Cherries Jubilee

VEAL BIRDS

1 (8-ounce) can mushrooms,
  drained, or 1½ cups fresh
  mushrooms, chopped
2 tablespoons onion, minced
1 tablespoon butter
1 cup seasoned bread crumbs
1 tablespoon fresh parsley,
  chopped

2 teaspoons Worcestershire sauce
Salt and pepper
1 egg, slightly beaten
1 pound veal, thinly sliced
2 tablespoons flour
2 tablespoons shortening
1 can tomato soup
Parmesan cheese, grated

Saute' mushrooms and onions in butter. Add the bread crumbs, parsley, and Worcestershire sauce and season. Mix well and stir in egg. Place a portion of the stuffing on each slice of veal, roll up and secure with string. Coat the rolls with seasoned flour and fry in shortening until brown. Put the rolls in a casserole and pour the soup over them. Cover and bake 45 minutes at 350 degrees. Sprinkle liberally with Parmesan. Serves 4.

ASPARAGUS LOAF

¼ cup butter
1 cup crumbled crackers
2 eggs, beaten
2 cups warm milk
1 tablespoon grated onion

½ teaspoon salt
2 (15-ounce) cans green-tip
  asparagus, drained
1 can cream of asparagus soup
¼ cup milk

Melt butter in a skillet. Add crackers and stir until they begin to turn color. Mix together eggs, milk, onion, and salt. Add asparagus and crackers. Bake in a greased loaf pan at 350 degrees about 30 minutes, or until set. Heat the soup diluted with milk and pour over loaf to serve. In place of the asparagus soup, a combination of cream of mushroom soup, ¼ cup milk, and ½ cup melted American cheese may be used as a sauce. Serves 6—8.

CHARLIE'S CHOCOLATE MOUSSE

2 squares unsweetened chocolate
½ cup sugar
¼ cup water
4 eggs, separated
1 cup soft butter

1¼ cups powdered sugar
1 teaspoon vanilla
2 teaspoons Kahlua (optional)
½ pint whipping cream, whipped
Lady Fingers

Heat in a double boiler chocolate, sugar, and water. Add slightly beaten egg yolks. Cook, stirring, until smooth. Cool. Cream butter and powdered sugar, and add to cooked mixture, blending well. Add vanilla and Kahlua. Fold in whipped cream, reserving enough for decorating servings. Fold in stiffly beaten egg whites. Pile into a spring-form pan lined with Lady Fingers. Chill 24 hours. Serves 6.

BLIND FINCHES

6 lean, thin beef or veal steaks
¼ pound lean pork (6 thin slices)
Salt and pepper

6 dill gherkins
6 tablespoons butter
¼ cup water

Salt and pepper the steaks and place the pork slices on them. Roll a gherkin up in each steak. Secure them with a toothpick. Brown in butter, then add water to make a thin gravy. Simmer for one hour. Serves 6.

CREOLE CUCUMBERS

4 large cucumbers, washed and
    split lengthwise
2 tablespoons onion, chopped
2 tablespoons parsley, chopped

4 tablespoons butter
1 cup bread crumbs
1 cup tomato pulp
Salt and pepper

Scoop out seed portion of cucumbers and save. Boil the cucumbers in lightly salted water for about 10 minutes. Drain. Saute onion and parsley in butter. Add other ingredients and the reserved cucumber pulp and cook, stirring, for 5 minutes. Fill cucumber shells with the stuffing and place in a shallow baking dish. Add a small amount of water and bake at 350 degrees for 15 minutes, or until brown on top. Serves 8.

MOCK CHICKEN SALAD

1 package plain gelatin
¼ cup water
1¾ cups hot chicken broth
1 (8½-ounce) can small peas,
  partially drained

½ cup celery, chopped
¼ cup stuffed olives, sliced
1 hard-cooked egg, chopped
½ cup pecans, chopped
Mayonnaise

Soften gelatin in ¼ cup cold water. Dissolve gelatin in hot broth. Cool. Add the other ingredients and chill until set. Garnish with mayonnaise. Serves 6.

CHERRIES JUBILEE

1 tablespoon cornstarch
1 teaspoon cold water
1 (16-ounce) can dark cherries,
  drained

2 tablespoons sugar
½ cup brandy
Vanilla ice cream

Dissolve cornstarch in water. Add sugar and liquid drained from cherries. Cook, stirring, until thick and transparent. Pour over cherries. Add brandy and light with a match. Stir as flame burns. Pour over ice cream. Serves 4–6.

On the Fifth Day of Christmas,

my true love gave to me, five golden rings.

Not 24-carat, but carrots molded in a ring for a bridge luncheon. There will be plenty of time to find the cards and tallies since most of the cooking must be done beforehand.

BRIDGE LUNCHEON

Chicken à la Reine on Cranberry Ring
Vertical Green Beans
Hot Rolls
Crème L'Orange
- or -
Onions on Cheese Toast
Carrot Ring
Golden Ring Slaw
Orange-Banana Ring

CHICKEN A LA REINE ON CRANBERRY RING

2 tablespoons gelatin
½ cup water
1 can cream of mushroom soup
8 ounces cream cheese
1 cup mayonnaise
2 teaspoons Worcestershire sauce
1 teaspoon salt

Few dashes white pepper
1 cup cooked chicken, chopped
1 cup celery, finely chopped
Salad greens
Jellied cranberry sauce
Homemade mayonnaise

Soften gelatin in ½ cup cold water. In top of double boiler, heat and blend well the soup and cream cheese. Stir in and mix well 1 cup mayonnaise, Worcestershire sauce, salt and pepper. Add gelatin and stir until dissolved. Fold in chicken and celery. Pour into muffin tins that have been rinsed in cold water. Chill until set. Serve on a slice of cranberry jelly on a bed of fresh greens. Top with mayonnaise. Serves 8—10.

VERTICAL GREEN BEANS

2 cans vertical-pack green beans
2 slices-bacon
½ cup brown sugar

Butter
Garlic salt

Drain and rinse beans in cold water. Arrange in a buttered baking dish. Cut bacon into small pieces and place on beans. Sprinkle brown sugar on top and a few shakes of garlic salt. Dot with butter. Bake uncovered at 350 degrees, stirring often until beans are cooked. Serves 8.

CREME L'ORANGE

2 tablespoons plain gelatin
½ cup cold water
½ cup boiling water
1 cup sugar
1½ cups orange juice and pulp

4 tablespoons lemon juice
3 egg whites
¼ teaspoon salt
½ pint whipping cream, whipped
2 oranges, thinly sliced

Soften gelatin in cold water. Stir until dissolved in boiling water. Add sugar, orange juice, pulp and lemon juice. Chill until nearly set. Beat until foamy. Beat egg whites and salt until stiff. Fold into gelatin. Fold in the whipped cream. Pour into a mold that has been rinsed in cold water. Chill. Serve garnished with orange slices. Serves 6.

Fifth Day of Christmas

ONIONS ON CHEESE TOAST

6 medium onions
4 tablespoons butter
4 tablespoons flour
1¾ cups milk
¼ cup water in which onions

were cooked
Salt and pepper
Cheddar cheese, sliced
12 slices whole wheat bread,
toasted and buttered

Cook onions until soft in small amount of lightly salted water. Make cream sauce with butter, flour, milk, and onion water. Add onions and season. Place cheese on toasted bread. Spoon creamed onions over cheese slices. Serves 6.

CARROT RING

2 eggs
1 cup milk
½ cup almonds, sliced
1 teaspoon sugar

½ teaspoon salt
2½ cups shredded carrots
3 tablespoons butter

Beat eggs. Add milk, almonds, seasoning, and carrots. Melt butter in the mold to grease it and then drain the rest into the carrot mixture. Pour the mixture into the mold and place the mold in a pan of hot water and cook 45 minutes or until done in 350-degree oven. Unmold on platter. The center may be filled with English peas. Serves 6

GOLDEN RING SLAW

3 tablespoons lime juice
3 tablespoons sour cream
2 tablespoons mayonnaise
4 cups finely shredded cabbage
1 tablespoon sugar

¼ teaspoon salt
Few dashes pepper
1 (11-ounce) can mandarin orange
segments, drained

Blend together the lime juice, sour cream and mayonnaise. Stir into cabbage. Sprinkle on the sugar, salt and pepper and toss. Top with a ring of the orange segments. Serves 6.

ORANGE-BANANA RING

1 package orange gelatin
1½ cups boiling water
¼ cup sugar
Few grains of salt
½ cup orange juice

1 tablespoon lemon juice
1½ cups bananas, sliced
½ pint whipping cream, whipped
Lady Fingers

Dissolve gelatin in boiling water. Add sugar, salt, orange juice and lemon juice. Chill until mixture begins to thicken. Fold in bananas and whipped cream. Pour into a spring-form pan lined with Lady Fingers. Chill. Serves 6.

On the Sixth Day of Christmas,

my true love gave to me, six geese a-laying.

These six geese are laying eggs, so today is perfect for a brunch. You can use store-bought patty shells and you don't have to prepare your ham, but if you would like to try your hand at something different, here are the recipes.

BRUNCH

Pâté
Egg Cutlets
Jacqueline's Curried Peas and Shrimp in Patty Shells
Peach 'a la Chutney
- or -
Oeufs-Crevettes
Ham
Nut Biscuits
Brandied Figs

PATE

2 cups chicken livers
Brandy
1 cup fat from sliced bacon,
    minced
1 small clove garlic, crushed

½ teaspoon dill weed
1 tablespoon onion, minced
1 tablespoon salt
1 bay leaf

Soak chicken livers in brandy in refrigerator for 3 days. Mince chicken livers and blend thoroughly with remaining ingredients except bay leaf. Place in earthenware mold or bowl, put bay leaf on top, and cover with foil. Place mold in pan with shallow water and bake at 300 degrees 3 hours. Cool thoroughly and refrigerate for a day before serving. Serve with hot buttered toast. Serves 6.

EGG CUTLETS

2 tablespoons butter
4 tablespoons flour
1 cup milk
8 hard-cooked eggs, chopped
1 teaspoon onion, finely chopped
1 teaspoon parsley, minced

½ teaspoon paprika
Salt and pepper
Flour
1 egg, beaten
Cracker crumbs

Make cream sauce with first three ingredients. Add hard-cooked eggs, onion, parsley, paprika, salt and pepper. Cool and shape into cutlets. Dip in flour, beaten egg, and cracker crumbs. Fry in deep fat. Serves 6.

JACQUELINE'S CURRIED PEAS AND SHRIMP IN PATTY SHELLS

3½ tablespoons butter
3½ tablespoons flour
1½ cups milk
1½ teaspoons salt
½ teaspoon white pepper
¼ teaspoon cayenne
1 scant teaspoon curry powder

2 (17-ounce) cans early English
    peas, heated and drained
1 (2½-ounce) can mushrooms,
    drained
3 tablespoons pimientos, drained
    and minced
2 cups shrimp, cooked and cut
    in half

Make a cream sauce with the butter, flour, and milk. Add seasoning. Gently fold in vegetables and shrimp. Heat in a double boiler for 15 minutes, stirring often. Serve in patty shells. Serves 8—10.

Sixth Day of Christmas

PUFF PASTRY

1½ cups flour   *1 cup butter, cold and firm*
½ teaspoon salt   *Water with a squeeze of lemon*

Sift flour and salt into a bowl. Cut the butter in ½-inch cubes. Add to flour. Mix to a stiff dough with cold lemon water. Roll into a rectangle on floured board to 1-inch thickness. Brush off loose flour. Fold 1/3 of dough on top and another 1/3 underneath so that the ends are on opposite sides. Give the pastry a half turn and repeat rolling and folding. Refrigerate for 20 minutes. Roll and fold twice, refrigerate. Repeat twice. Roll and cut and refrigerate before baking.

PATTY SHELLS

Roll puff pastry 1/8-inch thick and cut with donut cutter with center cutter removed from base of shell. For top, cut as for a donut. Turn bottom round over before placing on a moistened baking sheet. Moisten one side of top ring and place on base. Prick the centers and refrigerate for 20 minutes. Bake at 475 degrees about 12 minutes or until shells are golden. The dough can be frozen after the rolling and folding procedure. Makes about 2 dozen.

PEACH A LA CHUTNEY

Canned peach halves   *Butter*
Chutney

Place peach halves in a baking dish. Fill the centers with chutney and dot with butter. Bake at 400 degrees until just hot.

OEUFS-CREVETTES

For each serving:

1 teaspoon butter   *1 tablespoon cream*
3 or 4 shrimp, cooked and peeled   *1 tablespoon Swiss cheese, grated*
1 egg   *Salt and pepper*

Melt butter in ramekin or custard cup. Add shrimp. Break egg over shrimp. Season. Pour on cream and top with cheese. Bake at 400 degrees for 8–10 minutes.

Sixth Day of Christmas

HOME-CURED HAM

Place the ham in a large container of water (the ham should be well covered with the water). Leave for 24 hours. Drain. On the second day, mix ¾ quart of cider vinegar with one pound of dark brown sugar, and water to cover the ham. Cook in this mixture 18 minutes to the pound. Let the ham stand in the liquid overnight. On the third day, remove the skin from the ham. Score the ham and cover with a mixture of 1¾ cups corn meal, ½ pound dark brown sugar, 2 teaspoons dry mustard, and 1 cup dry sherry. Bake at 350 degrees until glaze hardens.

NUT BISCUITS

2 cups flour
4 teaspoons baking powder
¾ teaspoon salt
2 tablespoons butter

½ cup pecans, ground
½ cup plus 2 tablespoons milk
Butter, melted

Sift dry ingredients. Cut in butter. Mix in nuts. Make a hole in center and add milk slowly. Stir from the center slowly until a soft dough has been formed. Roll gently on floured board and press with palm of hand to ¼-inch thickness. Cut into small rounds, brush with butter, and place one round on top of another. Bake on ungreased cookie sheet at 400 degrees 15 minutes or until lightly brown. Makes about 18 biscuits.

BRANDIED FIGS

4 cups figs
Pinch of baking soda
3 cups water

3 cups sugar
1 lemon
Brandy

Wash figs in water to which has been added a small amount of baking soda. Rinse and place in colander. Bring sugar and water to a boil in a large enamel boiler. Add a whole lemon, thinly sliced and seeded. Drop in figs and cook until clear. As the figs cook, stir frequently and wash down the sugar crystals from the side of the pan with a brush dipped in cold water. Allow the figs to "rest" in the syrup overnight. Next day remove figs to a platter and cook the syrup until thickened. Return the figs to the syrup and bring to a boil. Remove from heat and ladle into sterilized jars. Add one tablespoon of brandy to each jar. Seal with lid. Makes about 4 jars.

Sixth Day of Christmas

On the Seventh Day of Christmas,

my true love gave to me, seven swans a-swimming.

Swans swim and one has a fish in its mouth! Instead of fried swan, let's feature seafood for a cocktail buffet. Many of the dishes should be prepared the day before. Make your own selection.

COCKTAIL BUFFET

Oysters Rockefeller Dip
Courtbouillon
Crabmeat au Gratin
Oysters Bienville
Vegetable Festival
Stuffed Bacon Rolls
Scandinavian Meat Balls
Cheese Ball
Shrimp Rolls
Pumpkin Pickle D'Or
Assorted Party Crackers, Chips, and
Small Pastry Shells

OYSTERS ROCKEFELLER DIP

2 packages frozen chopped
    spinach
¾ stick butter
2 tablespoons grated onion
1 clove garlic, crushed

Tabasco
Salt and pepper
2 pints oysters
1 cup bread crumbs
Parmesan cheese

Cook spinach and drain thoroughly. Melt butter. Add seasoning. Drain oysters and blot with a towel. Mix melted butter gently with spinach. Add bread crumbs and oysters and stir gently. Place in a greased casserole and sprinkle with cheese. Cover and bake at 350 degrees for 30 minutes, then uncovered for 15 minutes. Serve with Melba rounds.

COURTBOUILLON

6 pounds of fish (red snapper,
    red fish or catfish)
½ cup oil
¼ cup flour
2 large onions, sliced
1 (16-ounce) can tomatoes
2 bay leaves
4 green peppers, sliced
4 shallots, chopped

1 clove garlic, chopped
¼ teaspoon allspice
¼ cup catsup
1 cup water
1 teaspoon parsley
2 slices lemon
½ cup claret wine
1 teaspoon port wine

Cut fish into pieces. Stir flour in oil until slightly brown. Add onions and brown. Add tomatoes and cook 5 minutes. Add remaining ingredients except wine and fish. Cook 30 minutes. Add the fish and simmer 20 minutes. Add wine and bring to a boil. Serves 8–10.

CRABMEAT AU GRATIN

2 tablespoons onion, finely
　chopped
1 bell pepper, chopped
4 tablespoons butter
4 tablespoons flour
1 cup milk
2 egg yolks, slightly beaten
½ pint sour cream

1 teaspoon parsley, minced
2 tablespoons lemon juice
1 (2-ounce) jar pimiento, chopped
½ teaspoon Worcestershire sauce
Salt and white pepper
1 pound crabmeat
1 cup Swiss cheese, grated

Saute onions and bell pepper in butter until tender. Add flour and cook, stirring, for 2 minutes. Add milk and stir until mixture thickens. Remove from heat and blend in egg yolks and sour cream. Add parsley, lemon juice, pimiento, Worcestershire, salt and pepper. Fold in crabmeat and cheese. Bake in greased casserole at 375 degrees for 30 minutes. Serves 6.

OYSTERS BIENVILLE

2 dozen oysters
1 bunch shallots, chopped
3 tablespoons butter
3 tablespoons flour
½ cup chicken broth
½ cup shrimp, chopped
½ cup mushrooms, chopped

1 egg yolk
½ cup white wine
Salt and pepper
Bread crumbs
Parmesan cheese
Ice cream salt

Place oysters on half shell on ice cream salt in pie or cake pan. If you have no shells, place oysters directly in greased pie or cake pans. Bake at 350 degrees until partially done, about 6–8 minutes. Saute shallots in butter until brown. Add flour and stir until brown. Add chicken broth, shrimp, and mushrooms. Beat egg yolk with wine and add slowly to sauce, stirring constantly. Season. Simmer 10 to 15 minutes, stirring. Pour sauce over oysters, then cover with mixture of bread crumbs and cheese. Brown at 400 degrees about 12 minutes. Serves 4.

VEGETABLE FESTIVAL

Thinly sliced:
  yellow squash
  zucchini
  bell pepper
  radishes
  white onion
  red onion
  mushrooms
  turnip root

Sticks of:
  carrots
  celery
Cauliflower, cut up
1 cup olive oil
1¼ cups vinegar
¼ cup sugar
2 teaspoons salt
½ teaspoon pepper
1 clove garlic, minced

Bring oil, vinegar, and seasoning to a boil. Cool for 3 minutes. Mix in raw vegetables and chill overnight.

STUFFED BACON ROLLS

1 teaspoon onion, minced
1 stick butter
1 package stuffing mix

1 egg, well beaten, plus enough
  milk to measure 1 cup
Bacon

Sauté onion in butter. Stir in stuffing mix. Remove from heat. Add liquid and mix thoroughly. Wrap one full teaspoon in ½ strip bacon. Place on ungreased baking sheet and bake at 450 degrees until bacon cooks.

SCANDINAVIAN MEAT BALLS

1 pound round steak, ground
  twice
¼ pound blue cheese
1 teaspoon salt
Few dashes pepper

Few dashes mace
3 tablespoons flour
2 eggs
1½ cups light cream
3 tablespoons sherry

Mix thoroughly meat, cheese, salt, pepper, mace, flour. Beat in eggs one at a time. Add cream and sherry gradually, beating until light. Shape into balls and fry in butter until done. Makes about 2 dozen.

CHEESE BALL

½ pound sharp cheese
½ pound blue cheese
½ pound cheddar cheese
6 ounces Swiss cheese
1 pound cream cheese
2 pounds cheese spread (like
  Cheez-Whiz)

4 tablespoons Worcestershire
  sauce
1 teaspoon cayenne pepper
3 medium-size cloves of garlic.
  finely chopped
1 cup fresh parsley, finely
  chopped
2 cups pecans, chopped

Blend all the ingredients except the pecans. If necessary soften with a little mayonnaise. Shape into ball and roll in pecans. Wrap in foil and refrigerate overnight.

SHRIMP ROLLS

20 slices fresh white bread,
  crust removed
8 ounces cream cheese
1 cup shrimp (4½-ounce can)
2 tablespoons lemon juice

Few dashes seasoning salt
1 teaspoon onion, minced
½ clove garlic, minced
1 tablespoon mayonnaise
2 tablespoons sherry

Cut each slice of bread in half. Blend other ingredients well. Spread mixture on bread and roll up strip of bread. Place in pan, joined side down, cover with damp cloth and refrigerate overnight. Bake joined side down on baking sheet at 475 degrees for 5–10 minutes or until bread toasts. Makes 40 rolls.

PUMPKIN PICKLE D'OR

1 (4-pound) pumpkin, peeled and
  cut into small cubes
3 pounds sugar
¾ quart cider vinegar

2 tablespoons broken stick
  cinnamon
1 tablespoon whole cloves

Tie spices in a cheesecloth (doubled) sack. Mix sugar and vinegar in a large boiler. Add the spices and bring to a boil. Add the pumpkin and cook until tender. Discard spices and ladle pumpkin into sterile jars. Fill to cover with syrup and seal. Makes 6 pints. Tie a bright green ribbon around jars for cheery Christmas gifts.

Seventh Day of Christmas

On the Eighth Day of Christmas,

my true love gave to me, eight maids a-milking.

Maids go a-milking early in the day, and so this party begins very early, in fact, the first hour of the eighth day. Midnight breakfast follows the singing of "Auld Lang Syne." Instead of milk, lots of fresh hot coffee will be in demand.

MIDNIGHT BREAKFAST

Quiche
Canadian Bacon
Cranberry Muffins

- or -

Velvet Scrambled Eggs
Sausage
Milk Fudge
Preserves

QUICHE

4 eggs
1 cup heavy cream
½ teaspoon salt
Cayenne pepper

6 slices bacon, chopped
1 (9-inch) unbaked pie shell
6 slices sharp cheddar cheese

Beat eggs and cream. Add seasonings and mix well. Place broiled, drained bacon on bottom of unbaked crust. Add thin cheese slices, then pour in eggs and cream. Bake at 400 degrees for 12—15 minutes. Reduce heat to 325 degrees and continue baking until firm, about 40 minutes. Serves 6.

CRANBERRY MUFFINS

1 egg, lightly beaten
¾ cup milk
2 cups flour
4 teaspoons baking powder
¼ cup sugar

½ teaspoon salt
½ stick butter, melted
1 cup cranberries
2 tablespoons sugar

Combine egg and milk. Sift together dry ingredients, except 2 tablespoons sugar, and add to egg and milk. Blend in butter. Roll the berries in 2 tablespoons sugar and fold into the batter. Bake in greased muffin tins at 375 degrees 30 minutes. Makes about 1 dozen muffins.

VELVET SCRAMBLED EGGS

8 eggs
4 teaspoons milk
4 tablespoons sour cream

½ teaspoon salt
White pepper
4 tablespoons butter

Mix together all the ingredients except the butter. Melt butter in a skillet and add eggs. Stir and cook to a desired consistency.

MILK FUDGE

3¼ cups self-rising flour
1 teaspoon baking powder

½ stick sweet butter (not mar-
garine)
1¼ cups milk

Mix flour and baking powder. Rub in butter. Make into dough with milk (a little extra may be needed). Divide into two portions. Roll out to about 1-inch thick. Bake on a greased baking sheet at 400 degrees about 25 minutes. Cut into squares. Makes about 2 dozen.

On the Ninth Day of Christmas,

my true love gave to me, nine ladies dancing.

And there are Sally and Charlotte and Mona Lisa and Granny all waiting for lunch!

LADIES LUNCHEON

Lady's Thighs
Spinach Madeleine
Queen's Caprice Salad
Granny Loaf
Simple Charlotte
- or -

Crème de Volaille
Steamed Broccoli
Orange-Piquante Salad
Sally Lunn
Pears Mona Lisa

LADY'S THIGHS

1 pound ground beef
2 tablespoons uncooked rice
3 eggs, (1 beaten with 1 teaspoon milk)
1 teaspoon olive oil
1 small onion, chopped

½ cup seasoned bread crumbs
1 teaspoon parsley, chopped
1 teaspoon dill weed, chopped
Salt and pepper
Cracker crumbs
2 tablespoons butter

Combine meat with rice, 2 eggs, olive oil, onion, bread crumbs, parsley, dill, and seasoning. Shape into small balls. Roll meatballs in beaten egg and milk, then in cracker crumbs. Melt butter in skillet and fry meatballs until golden brown. Serves 4–6.

SPINACH MADELEINE

2 packages frozen chopped spinach
4 tablespoons butter
4 tablespoons flour
Salt

2 cups milk
¼–½ cup dry white wine
Tabasco
¼ cup Parmesan cheese

Cook spinach according to directions. Drain thoroughly. Melt butter and add flour and salt. Cook, stirring, 2 minutes. Add milk gradually and stir until mixture thickens. Add wine, several drops of Tabasco and cheese. Blend into spinach. Bake in a greased casserole at 350 degrees for 10 minutes. This serves 6–8 as a casserole or can be used in a chafing dish as a dip.

QUEEN'S CAPRICE SALAD

1 tart apple, diced
1 cup celery, diced
6 fresh mushrooms, thinly sliced
1 grapefruit, sectioned, or 1 can grapefruit sections
1 tablespoon olive oil

½ teaspoon lemon juice
½ teaspoon salt
Endive or watercress, washed and blotted dry
Mayonnaise

Combine apple, celery, mushrooms and grapefruit with oil, lemon juice and salt. Arrange on a bed of greens. Garnish with fresh mayonaise. Serves 6.

GRANNY LOAF

3¼ cups self-rising flour
1 teaspoon baking powder
1 teaspoon pumpkin pie spice
½ stick butter
4 tablespoons sugar

3 ounces raisins (2 small boxes)
2 tablespoons candied peel,
  chopped
1¼ cups milk

Mix flour, baking powder, and spice. Rub in butter. Stir in sugar, raisins and peel. Make into dough with the milk. Turn onto a floured board and form a round. Place in a well-greased 8-inch round cake pan. Brush with a little milk. Bake at 400 degrees for about an hour.

SIMPLE CHARLOTTE

1 large bag marshmallows
¼ cup white rum
1 tablespoon rum flavoring

1 pint whipping cream, whipped
2 packages Lady Fingers
Dark chocolate, grated

Melt the marshmallows in the top of a double boiler. Cool. Fold the marshmallows and flavorings into the unsweetened whipped cream. Line a spring-form pan with Lady Fingers. Pour in the cream mixture and chill until very firm. Garnish with the grated chocolate. This can be frozen.

CREME DE VOLAILLE

1 chicken, boiled and deboned
1 (4-ounce) can mushrooms
3 tablespoons butter
2 tablespoons flour
1 cup milk
3 eggs, well beaten

1 tablespoon parsley, chopped
2 tablespoons onion, finely
  chopped
Salt and pepper
1 can cream of mushroom soup
½ pint sour cream

Grind or chop finely the chicken and ½ can of mushrooms. Melt 2 tablespoons butter and blend in flour. Add milk and stir till the sauce thickens. Remove from heat and add 1 tablespoon butter and the eggs. Blend thoroughly. Add parsley, onion, salt and pepper. Blend the sauce into the chicken and mushroom mixture. Put in a greased mold, cover with foil and place in pan of water. Bake at 350 degrees for 1½ hours or until knife inserted comes out clean. If individual molds are used, the cooking time will be shortened. Heat mushroom soup with sour cream and other ½ can of mushrooms. Serve as a sauce. Serves 6.

Ninth Day of Christmas

ORANGE-PIQUANTE SALAD

Oranges, peeled and thinly sliced
White onions, thinly sliced
Salad greens (include kale or
   watercress)
½ cup oil
¼ cup vinegar

Few dashes dry mustard
¼ teaspoon sugar
Few dashes paprika
½ teaspoon celery salt
Few shakes garlic powder
Cashew nuts

Arrange oranges and onions on bed of salad greens which have been tossed in some of the dressing made from remaining ingredients except nuts. Sprinkle nuts on top. Pour on remaining dressing.

SALLY LUNN

6 tablespoons butter
¼ cup sugar
1 large egg
1¾ cups flour

½ teaspoon salt
3 teaspoons baking powder
1 cup milk

Cream butter and sugar. Add well-beaten egg. Sift together flour, salt and baking powder. Add alternately with milk to creamed mixture. Bake in tiny greased muffin tins at 375 degrees about 20 minutes.

PEARS MONA LISA

6 pear halves (canned)
2 bars German sweet chocolate, melted

Vanilla ice cream
Individial meringues
½ pint whipping cream, whipped

Remove pear halves from syrup and allow to dry on a towel. Dip the pears into melted chocolate and place on ice cream on a meringue. Top with whipped cream.

MERINGUES

2 egg whites
Few grains of salt

½ cup plus 1 tablespoon sugar
½ teaspoon vanilla

Beat egg whites with salt until stiff but not dry. Gradually beat in sugar. Add flavoring. Spoon onto lightly greased baking sheet and bake at 225 degrees one hour or until quite dry. Store in tins. Makes about 6.

Ninth Day of Christmas

On the
Tenth Day
of Christmas,

my true love gave to me, ten lords a-leaping.

British lords! So here are British dinners. Let the lords leap while having a drink before dinner and later when the port goes round. The Lord Linlithgow's Soup is probably better for a summer menu, but we included it because we like it!

DINNER

Lord Ney's Bean Soup
Roast Beef
Creamy Horseradish Sauce
Yorkshire Pudding
Windsor Sprouts
English Trifle
- or -
Lord Linlithgow's Lebanese Soup
Roast Lamb and Gravy
Mint Sauce
Roasted Potatoes
Onion Sauce
London Peas
Steamed Jam Pudding with Custard Sauce

LORD NEY'S BEAN SOUP

2 cups navy beans
3 quarts water
6 slices bacon
3 large onions, cut in eighths

½ teaspoon Tabasco
4 stalks celery, chopped
Salt and pepper

Wash beans and remove any debris. Soak beans in cold water for one hour. Cut bacon into small pieces and fry until limp but not brown. Place all ingredients, including the bacon and bacon grease, in a large boiler and allow to simmer for about three hours. Serves 6.

ROAST BEEF

Before roasting the beef, make several small gashes and insert pieces of 2–3 cloves of garlic. Season with salt and pepper.

CREAMY HORSERADISH SAUCE

½ cup whipping cream, whipped

¼ cup cream-styled prepared horseradish

Blend thoroughly.

YORKSHIRE PUDDING

¾ cup self-rising flour
1 egg
1 cup milk

2 tablespoons drippings from roast, or vegetable oil

Make hole in center of flour. Put egg and ½ cup milk in center. Start mixing from center, working in all the flour. Add rest of milk. Heat fat in 7 x 11-inch baking pan. Pour in pudding and bake at 500 degrees for 10 minutes. Reduce heat to 425 degrees and bake for 30 minutes or until brown. Cut into squares. Serves 4.

WINDSOR SPROUTS

1 package frozen Brussels sprouts
2 tablespoons butter
2 tablespoons flour

¾ cups vegetable stock and milk
Dash of nutmeg or mace
Salt and pepper

Cook sprouts according to directions. Melt butter, stir in flour, and cook on low heat for 2 minutes. Blend in stock and milk and stir until thick. Season. Add sprouts. Serves 4.

Tenth Day of Christmas

ENGLISH TRIFLE

Red raspberry jam
Sponge cake
Sherry
Custard

Whipping cream, whipped and
  sweetened
Almonds, slivered

Spread jam on slices of sponge cake and place in serving dish. Drizzle a little sherry over cake. Cover with custard. Repeat these layers ending with custard. Spread whipped cream on top and garnish with almonds.

SPONGE CAKE

2 eggs
½ cup sugar

½ cup self-rising flour
½ teaspoon vanilla

Beat eggs until light. Add sugar and beat until thick and creamy. Fold flour in lightly, a little at a time. Add vanilla. Bake in well-greased and floured 8-inch round pan at 350 degrees about 30 minutes.

CUSTARD FOR TRIFLE

4 tablespoons flour
3 tablespoons sugar
½ teaspoon salt

2 cups milk
2 eggs, beaten
1 teaspoon vanilla

Make paste of flour, sugar, salt and a little of the milk. Bring rest of milk to boil and blend in paste, stirring constantly. Reduce heat and cook for 5 minutes. Remove from heat and beat in eggs. Cook, stirring, until thick. Add vanilla.

LORD LINLITHGOW'S LEBANESE SOUP

1 large cucumber
1 clove garlic, crushed
2 tablespoons tarragon vinegar
1 tablespoon gherkin, finely
  chopped

2 tablespoons mint, chopped
½ pint yogurt
½ pint heavy cream
½ cup shrimp or ½ avocado,
  sliced

Grate cucumber coarsely. Blend in blender with the remaining ingredients except the shrimp or avocado. Chill. Garnish with shrimp or avocado. Serves 6.

ROAST LAMB AND GRAVY

Salt and pepper the lamb and dredge it in flour. Place a large tablespoon of shortening on top, pour a little water in the pan and bake covered at 400 degrees 25 minutes per pound. Remove cover to brown—about 10—15 minutes. Remove from pan. Pour off some of the fat and brown flour in the rest. Stir in 1 cup boiling water with 1 beef bouillon cube to make gravy. More water may be needed. Season.

MINT SAUCE

¼ cup fresh mint, chopped　　　*¼ cup vinegar*
1 tablespoon sugar

Blend together in a blender 2 hours before serving.

ROASTED POTATOES

4 large baking potatoes　　　*1 stick butter*

Peel and cut potatoes into 6 pieces each. Parboil in salted water and drain. Melt butter in baking pan. Roll each piece of potato until covered in butter. Bake, turning to coat with butter at least twice, at 400 degrees about an hour, or until golden and crusty. Serves 6.

ONION SAUCE

2 onions, sliced　　　*½ cup milk*
½ cup water　　　*2 tablespoons water in which*
2 tablespoons butter　　　　*onions were cooked*
2 tablespoons flour　　　*Salt and pepper*

Cook onions in ½ cup lightly salted water until tender. Make cream sauce of flour, milk and onion water. Add onions and season.

LONDON PEAS

2 packages frozen English peas
2 cups chicken broth
1 tablespoon butter
2 tablespoons parsley, minced

1 tablespoon mint, minced
1 slice dry whole wheat bread,
   crumbled

Cook peas in broth. Blend in a blender 1/3 cup broth, seasoning, bread, and 1/3 cup peas. Pour sauce over rest of peas. Serves 8.

STEAMED JAM PUDDING

¾ cup flour
2 teaspoons baking powder
Few grains of salt
¼ cup sugar
2 tablespoons butter

1 egg
½ cup milk
1 teaspoon vanilla
4 tablespoons jam

Sift together flour, baking powder, salt, and sugar. Rub in butter. Beat egg and milk. Add vanilla. Blend dry mixture into egg and milk. Put jam at the bottom of a greased mold, pour in mixture, cover, place in a pan of water, and bake at 350 degrees for 1½ to 2 hours. Serve warm with custard sauce. Serves 4.

CUSTARD SAUCE

Same as Custard for Trifle except use only 2 tablespoons flour, 2 tablespoons sugar, and 1 egg.

Tenth Day of Christmas

On the Eleventh Day of Christmas,

my true love gave to me, eleven pipers piping.

The eleven pipers call to mind Scotland, and our Scottish recipes seem to be for tea food. If the eleventh day falls on Saturday or Sunday, invite whole families to tea. There are goodies to tempt all ages. Tea made properly is a real treat, not to be compared with the liquid produced by pouring tepid water over a tea bag! The children will probably want milk or a soft drink. Choose for yourself any two savories and two sweets—more of both as the guest list grows.

TEA

Pot of Tea	Ham-Egg-Mushroom Pie
Romanov Tea	Cream Scones
Spider Cider	Scotch Lace Wafers
Watercress Sandwiches	Fudge Brownies
Cucumber Sandwiches	Shortbread Toffee Squares
Egg and Olive Sandwiches	Cream Sponge
Open Orange Sandwiches	Dundee Cake
Kippers on Toast	Dundee Cream

Highland Mist

POT OF TEA

Heat tea pot with boiling water. Measure 1 full teaspoon of tea (try a mixture of Earl Grey and orange pekoe) for each cup plus 1 teaspoon for the pot. Pour boiling water over the tea and steep for 4 minutes. Serve with milk or lemon (and mint) and sugar. Be sure that the water is boiling!

ROMANOV TEA

10 whole cloves
10 whole allspice
3 sticks cinnamon
2 cups strong tea
1 large can frozen orange juice,
    diluted as directed

3 lemons, juice and rind
2 cups pineapple juice
2 cups sugar
2 cups water

Tie spices in cheesecloth bag and add to remaining ingredients. Simmer, do not boil, for 2 hours. Remove spices. Add more water as needed. Can be refrigerated and heated before serving. Makes about 12 cups.

SPIDER CIDER

2 quarts apple cider
½ cup brown sugar
Cinnamon sticks

1 teaspoon ground cloves
14–16 whole cloves

Bring sugar and cider to a boil and reduce immediately to a simmer. Tie 3 sticks of cinnamon and the other spices into a cheesecloth sack and add to liquid. Allow to simmer 15 minutes. Serve in mugs with a stick of cinnamon in each. Makes about 12 cups.

WATERCRESS SANDWICHES

½ cup butter
¾ cup watercress, finely chopped
¼ teaspoon salt

½ teaspoon lemon juice
2 drops Tabasco
8 slices bread

Cream butter. Add remaining ingredients. Spread on bread. Makes about 4 sandwiches.

CUCUMBER SANDWICHES

1 cucumber, thinly sliced　　　*Butter*
¼ cup vinegar　　　　　　　*Thin-sliced bread*
¾ cup water　　　　　　　　*Salt and pepper*

Soak cucumber in vinegar and water for an hour. Butter thin slices of bread and pile cucumber slices on bread. Season and cover with another piece of buttered bread. Makes about 4 sandwiches.

EGG AND OLIVE SANDWICHES

2 hard-cooked eggs, chopped　*Salt and pepper*
¼ cup stuffed olives, sliced　*Bread*
Mayonnaise

Lightly mix together eggs, olives, and mayonnaise. Season. Spread between slices of white or whole wheat bread.

OPEN ORANGE SANDWICHES

½ cup soft butter　　　　　*¼ teaspoon salt*
½ cup grated orange rind　　*Thin-sliced bread*
1 teaspoon orange juice

Cream the butter. Gradually beat in the rind and juice. Add salt. Spread on thinly sliced bread and serve open-faced. Makes about 4

KIPPERS ON TOAST

Rinse kippers under cold water. Poach in milk until tender. Serve on buttered toast.

HAM-EGG-MUSHROOM PIE

1 (9-inch) unbaked pie shell　　*1 cup fresh mushrooms, sliced,*
*　(use self-rising flour and omit*　*　or ½ cup canned mushroom*
*　salt)*　　　　　　　　　　*　pieces*
½ cup light cream　　　　　*½ cup cheese, grated*
4 eggs, beaten　　　　　　*Salt and white pepper*
4 slices ham, cut up

Make pie crust. Beat cream into eggs. Mix ham, mushrooms, and cheese and place in pie shell. Pour in eggs. Season. Bake at 425 degrees about 30 minutes. Serves 6–8.

Eleventh Day of Christmas

CREAM SCONES

2 cups flour
4 teaspoons baking powder
½ teaspoon salt
2 teaspoons sugar

4 tablespoons butter
2 eggs, well beaten (except for
   a small amount of 1 white)
½ cup cream

Mix the first four ingredients and cut in butter. Add eggs and cream. Roll to ¾-inch thickness. Cut out with biscuit cutter or cut in squares. Brush with saved egg white. Bake on ungreased baking sheet at 425 degrees for 12–15 minutes. Serve split and buttered or with cream cheese and strawberry jam. Makes about 2 dozen.

SCOTCH LACE WAFERS

2 cups oats
1 cup flour
2 teaspoons baking powder
½ teaspoon salt

½ cup sugar
3 tablespoons butter
¼ cup milk
½ teaspoon vanilla

Combine and mix well dry ingredients. Cut in butter. Add vanilla and add only enough milk to hold the ingredients together. Knead the dough well and roll out very thin. Cut with a small biscuit cutter and bake on a greased baking sheet at 375 degrees for 15–20 minutes. After cooling, the wafers will be crisp. Makes about 2 dozen.

FUDGE BROWNIES

3 tablespoons butter
1 cup sugar
2 eggs, beaten
2 squares unsweetened chocolate,
   melted

2 tablespoons flour
1 teaspoon vanilla
Few dashes salt
1 cup pecans, chopped

Cream butter, sugar, and a little of the beaten eggs. Beat in rest of egg. Blend in chocolate. Fold in flour. Add vanilla, salt, and nuts. Bake in greased pan at 325 degrees for 30 minutes. Makes about 3 dozen.

SHORTBREAD TOFFEE SQUARES

½ stick butter
4 tablespoons sugar
1 cup self-rising flour
½ stick butter
2 tablespoons sugar
1 (14-ounce) can condensed milk

¼ cup pecans, chopped
½ teaspoon vanilla
4 ounces German sweet chocolate, melted in 1 tablespoon
water

Cream ½ stick butter with 4 tablespoons sugar. Blend in flour. Spread onto greased 8-inch square pan, and bake at 350 degrees 20 minutes. Mix together next 4 ingredients and cook, stirring until mixture leaves the sides of the pan. Add vanilla. Pour over shortbread. Cool. Spread melted chocolate over toffee. Cool. Cut into squares. Makes about 12.

CREAM SPONGE

Make sponge cake given with Trifle. Split sponge and fill with jam and whipped cream. Dust top with powdered sugar.

DUNDEE CAKE

¾ cup butter
¾ cup sugar
4 eggs
1½ cups flour
1 teaspoon baking powder
½ teaspoon salt

½ teaspoon pumpkin pie spice
¾ cup raisins
½ cup currants
½ cup candied peel, chopped
¾ cup almonds, chopped
1 teaspoon vanilla

Cream butter and sugar. Beat in eggs one at a time. Sift together flour, baking powder, salt and spice. Beat into butter mixture. Fold in fruit and half the nuts. Place the rest of the nuts on top of the cake. Bake in greased and floured loaf pan placed in a pan of shallow water at 325 degrees for 2 hours.

DUNDEE CREAM

2 eggs
2 egg yolks
3 tablespoons sugar
6 teaspoons brandy
2 cups milk, warmed

1 tablespoon butter, melted
1 teaspoon lemon peel, grated
Dundee Marmalade, melted with
  a little water
½ cup whipping cream, whipped

Beat eggs and egg yolks well. Beat in sugar and brandy. Stir butter into milk and blend with eggs and lemon peel. Pour into custard cups. Cover with foil. Place in a pan of shallow water, and bake at 325 degrees for about 25 minutes, or until set. When cool, turn out of cups and pour marmalade over custard. Garnish with whipped cream. Serves 6.

HIGHLAND MIST

1 (8-ounce) can crushed pineapple
8–10 macaroons, crumbled
½ pint whipping cream

1 teaspoon vanilla
1 tablespoon powdered sugar
½ cup pecans, chopped

Drain pineapple, reserving liquid. Mix macaroon crumbs with pineapple juice to form paste. Whip cream, adding vanilla and powdered sugar. Make layers in casserole of paste, pineapple, and cream. Garnish with nuts. Chill. Serves 6.

On the Twelfth Day of Christmas,

my true love gave to me, twelve drummers drumming.

Twelve drummers drum for the Twelfth Night Revels. Music may be "the food of love" in Shakespeare's play, but we had better attend to something more substantial to feed our revellers. If one is very clever or artistic, one may decorate the cakes to look like drums. Some may have to rely upon drumsticks alone for the motif. As for the menu, "What You Will!"

TWELFTH NIGHT REVELS

Eggnog
Champagne Punch
Wassail Bowl
Drumsticks
Glazed Pork Tenderloin
Shrimp and Crab Casserole
Turkey Logs
Harlequin Spinach
Potatoes au Gratin

Corn and Pepper Casserole
Confetti Rice Salad
Macaroni Salad
Christmas Slaw
Aspic Elizabeth
Deviled Eggs
Aunt Bert's Rolls
Fruit Compote
Lazy Daisy Cake

EGGNOG

6 egg yolks
½ cup sugar
½ cup whiskey
6 egg whites

Pinch salt
2 pints whipping cream
Grated nutmeg

Beat egg yolks until light and fluffy. Beat in the sugar slowly. Continue beating while adding the whiskey. Whip egg whites until very stiff. Add pinch of salt. Fold the yolk mixture into the egg whites. Whip the cream. Fold in carefully. Serve with grated nutmeg. The whiskey measurement may be increased by one-half if preferred.

CHAMPAGNE PUNCH

12 lemons
Powdered sugar
1½ quarts carbonated water
¼ pint curacao

1½ pints brandy
2 quarts champagne
Block of ice

Squeeze the lemons and sweeten the juice with powdered sugar. Pour into a large punch bowl in which has been placed a block of ice. Add the carbonated water and liquors. If desired, a few cherries may be added for color. Makes 32 punch cups.

WASSAIL BOWL

1½ teaspoons nutmeg
1 teaspoon cinnamon
1 teaspoon allspice
3 cinnamon sticks, broken
12 cups water

10 tea bags
Sugar
14 jiggers bourbon
Lemons, sliced

Tie spices in a cheesecloth sack. Bring water to a boil. Add tea bags and the spice bag. Steep for 7 minutes. Sweeten to taste. Add bourbon. Serve with a slice of lemon floating in cup. Makes 26 punch cups.

DRUMSTICKS

3 dozen drumsticks cut from
   wings
Salt
2 eggs

½ cup water
2 cups flour
Cooking oil

Wash drumsticks and pat dry. Sprinkle with salt. Beat eggs lightly and blend in water. Place in a large bowl. Pour flour into another large bowl. Pour cooking oil into a heavy skillet to a depth of 1½ inches. Bring to a medium heat. Dip each drumstick in the egg batter and then roll in flour. Arrange in skillet. Do not crowd. Cover the skillet and cook until golden brown. Turn and cook in same fashion. Drain on brown paper.

GLAZED PORK TENDERLOIN

¾ cup brown sugar
2 tablespoons vinegar
2 teaspoons dry mustard
2 tablespoons cornstarch

¾ cup orange juice
1 (6-pound) tenderloin roast,
   deboned, rolled, and tied
Salt and pepper

Combine sugar, vinegar, mustard, cornstarch, and orange juice, and cook, stirring often, until mixture thickens. Wipe the roast well with a damp cloth, and rub with salt and pepper. Place on an oven rotisserie or an open rack and bake, basting with the glaze every 20 minutes, at 350 degrees until completely done (185—190 degrees).

SHRIMP AND CRAB CASSEROLE

2 cups milk
1 stick butter
½ cup flour
2 egg yolks, beaten
2 pounds shrimp, cooked and
   peeled

2 pounds crabmeat
Juice of 1 lemon
1 (8-ounce) can mushrooms
Salt
Cayenne
2 tablespoons sherry

Make cream sauce of milk, butter, and flour. Add 3 tablespoons of sauce to beaten yolks. Mix thoroughly. Blend eggs into rest of sauce. Cook, stirring, for 5 minutes. Add remaining ingredients. Bake in greased casseroles at 375 degrees for 20 minutes. Serves 8—10.

Twelfth Day of Christmas

TURKEY LOGS

½ stick butter
3 tablespoons flour
1 cup chicken broth
2 cups cooked turkey, diced
¼ cup celery, finely chopped
½ cup mushrooms, sliced
1 tablespoon pimiento, chopped

1 teaspoon salt
¼ teaspoon white pepper
Soft bread crumbs
1 egg, beaten
½ cup milk
Pecans or almonds, chopped

Melt butter and add flour. Cook, stirring, for 2 minutes. Add broth and stir until thick. Remove from heat and add next 6 ingredients. Season. Chill thoroughly. Divide into about 6 logs. Roll first in bread crumbs, then in egg mixed with milk, and finally in nuts. Fry in deep fat until golden brown. Serves 6.

HARLEQUIN SPINACH

2 packages frozen spinach
4 tablespoons butter
4 tablespoons flour
¾ cup milk
Tabasco

Salt and pepper
8 eggs
8 slices ham
8 slices Swiss cheese
2 tablespoons pimiento, chopped

Cook spinach according to directions. Drain well. Make cream sauce with butter, flour, and milk. Add few drops of Tabasco, ¼ teaspoon salt, and a little pepper. Spread spinach in greased baking pan. Cover with ham. Break an egg over each slice of ham. Season. Pour cream sauce over eggs. Cover with cheese. Sprinkle pimiento on top. Bake at 350 degrees about 20 minutes. Serves 8.

POTATOES AU GRATIN

2 cups potatoes, peeled and
   sliced
2 tablespoons butter
2 tablespoons flour

1 cup milk
1 cup cheese, grated
1 teaspoon Worcestershire sauce
Salt and pepper

Parboil potatoes in lightly salted water. Make cream sauce with butter, flour, and milk. Blend in cheese and Worcestershire sauce. Season. Bake at 425 degrees for 45 minutes. Serves 4—6.

CORN AND PEPPER CASSEROLE

2 cups creamed corn
½ cup bell pepper, chopped
1 cup soft bread crumbs
2 tablespoons butter, melted

1 teaspoon Worcestershire sauce
1 egg, well beaten
½ teaspoon salt
Few dashes pepper

Combine all ingredients and bake in greased casserole at 350 degrees for 20 minutes. Serves 6.

CONFETTI RICE SALAD

1 cup uncooked rice
½ teaspoon curry powder
½ cup mayonnaise
2 tablespoons liquid from sweet
    cucumber pickle
½ cup frozen whole kernel corn,
    cooked
½ cup frozen peas, cooked

¼ cup bell pepper, finely
    chopped
¼ cup celery, finely chopped
2 tablespoons onion, minced
¼ cup chutney
2 tablespoons raisins
¼ cup almonds, slivered

Boil rice in salted water until tender but not mushy. Drain well. Blend curry powder into mayonnaise and thin mixture with pickle vinegar. Mix thoroughly remaining ingredients with rice. Add mayonnaise and mix well. Chill thoroughly. Serves 10–12.

MACARONI SALAD

8 ounces elbow macaroni
½ cup cheese, diced
½ cup onion, chopped
½ cup celery, chopped
¼ cup bell pepper, chopped

2 tablespoons pimiento, chopped
3 hard-cooked eggs, chopped
¼ cup cucumber pickle, chopped
Salt
Mayonnaise

Cook macaroni according to directions. Add all ingredients except mayonnaise while macaroni is warm. Season. Cool. Add mayonnaise and mix thoroughly. Chill. Serves 6–8.

CHRISTMAS SLAW

½ cup red cabbage, shredded
1 head green cabbage, shredded
1 cup watercress, chopped
4 tablespoons olive oil
1 tablespoon lemon juice

1 clove garlic, crushed
2 tablespoons sour cream
2 tablespoons sugar
Salt and pepper
1 tart apple, chopped

Soak cabbage and watercress in lightly salted water for 5 minutes. In a blender, blend oil and lemon juice. Blend in remaining ingredients except apple. Lightly toss cabbage, watercress, and apple in dressing. Chill. Serves 8—10.

ASPIC ELIZABETH

4 cups V-8 juice
2½ tablespoons gelatin
1½ tablespoons lemon juice
1 tablespoon onion juice
Salt
½ teaspoon cayenne
2 teaspoons Worcestershire sauce

Tabasco
1 cup celery, finely chopped
1 cup bell pepper, finely chopped
Cream cheese and chopped pecans
   or shrimp
   or artichoke hearts
   or deviled eggs

Sprinkle gelatin over 1 cup cold V-8 juice. Bring remaining V-8 juice to a quick boil. Add lemon juice, onion juice, salt, cayenne, Worcestershire sauce, and Tabasco. Pour hot juice over gelatin mixture and stir until gelatin dissolves. Pour into individual molds and chill until partially set. Add celery, bell pepper and balls of cream cheese and pecans, or shrimp, etc. Chill thoroughly. Serves 8—10.

DEVILED EGGS

6 hard-cooked eggs
1 teaspoon prepared mustard
Salt and white pepper

Mayonnaise
Paprika

Mash yolks with mustard, salt and pepper. Add enough mayonnaise to make creamy but not soupy. Fill egg whites. Sprinkle paprika over top.

AUNT BERT'S ROLLS

1 package dry yeast
1¼ cups lukewarm water
¼ cup sugar
1 egg, beaten

1 teaspoon salt
½ cup shortening
4 cups flour

Dissolve yeast in water in a large mixing bowl. Add other ingredients and mix well. Cover with a towel and let rise in a warm place. When the dough seems to have doubled in size, punch down and refrigerate. Roll out and shape into rolls about 2 hours before baking in greased pans at 400 degrees about 15 minutes, or until golden. Makes about 4 dozen.

FRUIT COMPOTE

4 oranges
1 cup fruit juice
1 (16-ounce) can pears
1 (16-ounce) can sliced peaches
1 (16-ounce) can pineapple
    chunks
1 (16-ounce) can Queen Anne
    cherries
¾ cup sugar
¼ teaspoon salt

3 tablespoons butter
3 tablespoons flour
¾ cup sherry
½ pint whipping cream, whipped

For crunchy topping (optional):

1 cup flour
1 cup dark brown sugar
1 stick butter

Slice oranges into thin sections and simmer in fruit juice until tender. Drain the fruit, reserving the juice. Mix oranges with canned fruit and add sugar and salt. Melt butter and stir in flour. Add fruit juice and sherry and cook, stirring until thickened. Pour sauce over fruit. Bake at 375 degrees for 30–40 minutes. Garnish with lightly sweetened whipped cream. For a crunchy topping, combine flour and brown sugar. Cut in butter and sprinkle over the fruit before baking. Serves 24.

LAZY DAISY CAKE

2¼ cups self-rising flour
1¼ cups sugar
1 stick butter

1 cup milk
1 teaspoon vanilla
2 eggs

Sift flour and sugar together. Add butter, cut up, and ¾ cup of milk and beat for 2 minutes. Beat in rest of milk, vanilla, and eggs, one at a time. Beat for 2 minutes. Bake in 2 greased and floured 9-inch cake pans at 350 degrees for about 30 minutes.

Choose from these fillings and frostings:

LEMON CURD FILLING

3 eggs
2 lemons, juice and rind

1 cup sugar
½ stick butter

Beat eggs slightly and cook with other ingredients in top of double boiler until mixture thickens.

CHOCOLATE FILLING

1 can sweetened condensed milk
2 squares unsweetened chocolate

1 teaspoon vanilla
Pinch of salt

Cook milk and chocolate in double boiler until chocolate is melted. Add salt and vanilla.

DATE FILLING

2 cups dates
4 tablespoons water
2 tablespoons honey or syrup
2 teaspoons cornstarch

2 tablespoons cold water
2 tablespoons lemon flavoring
1 teaspoon vanilla

Cook dates in 4 tablespoons water until soft. Add honey. Mix cornstarch with 2 tablespoons cold water and stir into dates. Cook, stirring, 5 minutes. Add flavorings.

BUTTER FROSTING

½ stick butter
1½ cups powdered sugar
Few grains of salt

4 tablespoons milk
1 teaspoon vanilla

Melt butter. Beat in sugar, salt, and enough milk to soften. Add vanilla.

CHOCOLATE FROSTING

Same ingredients as Butter Frosting plus 4 tablespoons cocoa. Make a thick paste of cocoa and about 2–3 tablespoons boiling water. Beat into butter-sugar mixture before adding vanilla.

LEMON FROSTING

Use lemon juice instead of milk in Butter Frosting, and only ½ teaspoon vanilla.

INDEX

Shortbread Toffee Squares, 65
Simple Charlotte, 53
Sponge Cake, 57
Steamed Jam Pudding, 59

EGGS

Deviled Eggs, 72
Egg Cutlets, 38
Ham-Egg-Mushroom Pie, 63
Oeufs-Crevettes, 39
Quiche, 48
Velvet Scrambled Eggs, 48

HORS D'OEUVRES, SANDWICHES

Cheese Ball, 45
Cucumber Sandwiches, 63
Drumsticks, 69
Egg and Olive Sandwiches, 63
Open Orange Sandwiches, 63
Oyster Rockefeller Dip, 42
Pâte', 38
Scandinavian Meat Balls, 44
Shrimp Rolls, 45
Stuffed Bacon Rolls, 44
Vegetable Festival, 44
Watercress Sandwiches, 62

MEAT

Blind Finches, 31
Doves With Bacon, 20
Glazed Pork Tenderloin, 69
Ham-Egg-Mushroom Pie, 63
Home-Cured Ham, 40
Lady's Thighs, 52
Roast Beef, 56
Roast Lamb and Gravy, 58
Tournedos, 18
Veal Birds, 30

POULTRY

Chicken 'a la Reine, 34
Crème de Volaille, 53
Roast Quail, 12
Roast Turkey with Cornbread
    Dressing, 8
Turkey Logs, 70

PRESERVES, SAUCES

Brandied Figs, 40
Creamy Horseradish Sauce, 56
Custard Sauce, 59
Hard Sauce, 12
Mayonnaise For Sure, 14
Mint Sauce, 58
Onion Sauce, 58
Parsley Butter, 18
Pumpkin Pickle D'Or, 45
Salad Dressing. 18

SALADS

Aspic Elizabeth, 71
Avocado and Grapefruit Salad, 21
Christmas Slaw, 71
Confetti Rice Salad, 71
Cranberry-Pear Salad, 10
Golden Ring Slaw, 35
Macaroni Salad, 71
Mock Chicken Salad, 32
Molded Cranberry Salad, 14
Orange-Piquante Salad, 54
Queen's Caprice Salad, 52

SEAFOOD

Courtbouillon, 42
Crabmeat au Gratin, 43
Jacqueline's Curried Shrimp and
    Peas in Patty Shells, 38

Kippers, 63
Oysters Bienville, 43
Oysters Rockefeller Dip, 42
Shrimp and Crab Casserole, 69

SOUPS

Lord Linlithgow's Lebanese
  Soup, 57
Lord Ney's Bean Soup, 56
Mock Turtle Soup, 19
Turtle Soup, 17

VEGETABLES

Asparagus Loaf, 30
Broccoli Casserole, 13
Carrot Ring, 35

Cheese Grits, 20
Corn and Pepper Casserole, 71
Creole Cucumbers, 31
Dirty Rice, 13
Green Beans Almondine, 20
Green Beans and Celery, 9
Harlequin Spinach, 70
Holiday Sweet Potatoes, 9
London Peas, 59
Onions and Peas, 18
Onions on Cheese Toast, 35
Parsleyed Carrots, 13
Potatoes au Gratin, 70
Roasted Potatoes, 58
Spinach Madeleine, 52
Vertical Green Beans, 34
Windsor Sprouts, 56

The Quail Ridge Press "Best of the Best" Series:

Best of the Best from Louisiana $12.95   0-937552-13-5
Best of the Best from Texas $14.95   0-937552-14-3
Best of the Best from Florida $12.95   0-937552-16-X
Best of the Best from Mississippi $9.95   0-937552-09-7

The Quail Ridge Press Cookbook Series:

The Little Gumbo Book $6.95   0-937552-17-8
Hors D'Oeuvres Everybody Loves $4.95   0-937552-11-9
The Seven Chocolate Sins $4.95   0-937552-01-1
A Salad A Day $4.95   0-937552-02-X
Quickies For Singles $4.95   0-937552-03-8
The Twelve Days of Christmas Cookbook $4.95 5.95 0-937552-00-3
The Country Mouse Cheese Cookbook $4.95   0-937552-10-0
Any Time's A Party! $4.95   0-937552-12-7

Send check or money order or VISA/MasterCard number with expiration date to:

Quail Ridge Press
P. O. Box 123
Brandon, MS 39042

Please add $1.50 postage and handling for first book; $0.50 per additional book. Gift wrap with enclosed card add $1.25. Mississippi residents add 6% sales tax.